# #BOSSNOTES

A Quarterly Branding & Business Journal

Printed in the United States of America


First Printing, 2016


Alease Michelle Studio, LLC
PO Box 38013
Rock Hill, SC 29732


www.aleasemichelle.com/bossnotes

# CONTENTS

# #BOSSNOTE from Alease

Success is a mental game. You have to be your best mentally in order to achieve the things you want the most. You have to adopt a success mindset that allows you have the best outlook possible at any given time.

A success mindset can take you and your business to new levels of achievement, success and all the rewards that come along with reaching the goals that you set for yourself.

The thing is that while success is a mental game, your mental health is not. The health of the mind is intimately tied to the health of the body. In fact, the mind is so intimately tied to the body that, in some sense, they are one mechanism. If one part of the mechanism isn't functioning properly the entire system becomes less efficient. If the malfunction is serious enough, the entire system can crash.

This is why all truly successful people have learned how to implement success habits into their daily lives. Successful people understand that good habits lead to increased mental health and efficiency. This, in turn, allows them to operate at an exceptionally high levels.

In other words, someone who is operating at this level is nearly unstoppable. The bottom line is that you can't forget about your daily habits if you truly want to succeed and reach your goals.

To Your Success,

*Alease*

**FB** – www.facebook.com/aleasemichellefan    **IG** – www.Instagram.com/aleasemichelle

# IF YOU WANT TO BE SUCCESSFUL, IT'S JUST THIS SIMPLE. KNOW WHAT YOU ARE DOING. LOVE WHAT YOU ARE DOING. AND BELIEVE IN WHAT YOU ARE DOING.

Will Rogers

# SUCCESS HABITS TO POWER UP YOUR DAY

Things Successful People Do Each Morning in the First 2 Hours Before Checking their Email or Facebook

W e all know that habits can either help or hurt your success in life. Bad habits can fester and grow into a lifestyle that takes you away from the things you want to do and good habits can help you create a life that's full of action and accomplishment.

If you were to look at someone you respect, someone who's successful, you would see that they spend each day doing the things that help them accomplish their biggest goals. This isn't to say they're perfect—because no one is—but despite the things that are not perfect in their lives, they continue to make moves that have a positive impact. And it starts with their daily success habits.

Anyone can study successful habits. But it's worthless if you don't implement what you've learn. So, here are few ideas to help power up your day. Use them during your new two-hour morning routine or add them elsewhere to supercharge your productivity.

## Make Music Playlists to Fuel your Purpose

| Zen Playlist | Pumped up Gym Play | The Yoga Playlist: Rel | Ambient and Relaxing |
| Zen | Gym Playlists | Chakras Yoga Spécialist | Ambient |

Music can energize, galvanize and inspire. It can also calm, de-stress and soothe. Use energizing music when you are exercising or cleaning or sailing along through your tasks, getting them out the way.

Use soothing music when you need to de-stress or center yourself, such as during meditation.

Making separate playlists to suit your mood can really help make your day more productive.

## Honor Your Learning Style

Everyone has a predominant learning style, or even a mix of styles. Decide which type of learning is most effective for you:

- **Visual -** You find it easier to learn from graphics, videos, cartoons, diagrams, webinars or infographics.
- **Aural -**You'll pick an .MP3 file or a podcast over a webinar or article any day!
- **Kinesthetic -**You need to learn "hands on"—by doing things, touching them; jumping right into a new platform or software
- **Verbal -**You prefer the written word—transcripts, written instructions, articles—in fact, you can read an article faster than you can watch a video.

Once you have determined your best learning style or styles, honor it. Get rid of that written "To do" list if verbal learning is last on your preferences list. Dictate that article, if you're an aural learner. Draw little icon-pictures instead of writing things down or use a mind-map, if you're a visual learner.

If you cater to your preferred learning style(s) you will find that tasks flow easier and you remember things better, leaving you with more time, focus and energy.

**What is the most helpful idea from this section?**

_____

_____

_____

_____

_____

_____

## Just Say No

Ever find yourself in a reactive state, where your routine slips out of control? Chances are, you're agreeing to take on other tasks and responsibilities, when you should be saying "no".

Protect your routine by learning to respect your own boundaries. Never give excuses or reasons why you can't do something (this just encourages argumentative pressure). Just tell them "No. My plate is full."

## Automate Your Day

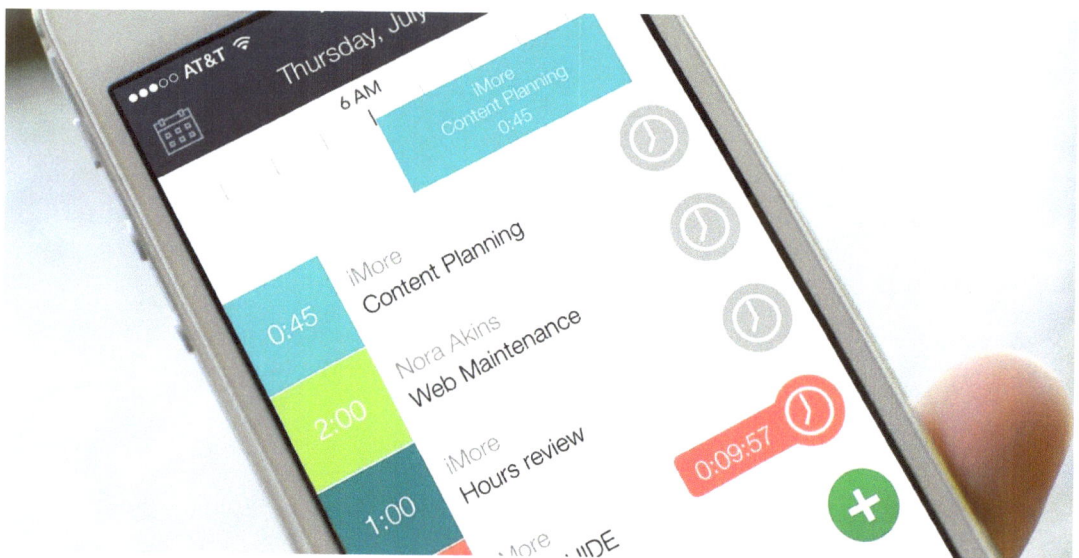

Why do something from scratch when you can automate it, using resources, apps, tools and templates?

Use timers, tracking apps, scheduling suites—whatever makes tasks easier for you or helps you perform tasks and take care of responsibilities more efficiently.

## Don't Sweat the Small Stuff

Throw out any task that isn't absolutely essential. If you can't throw it out, delegate or outsource it. That goes for household chores like cleaning—hire a cleaning lady—or grocery shopping too—many supermarkets allow you to order over the phone and have your groceries delivered.

## Don't Multi-task

No longer are women expected to be multi-tasking machines. Numerous studies now claim that multi-tasking reduces productivity and focus. A better idea: Plan your day ahead of time—either at the end of the day before, or in the morning as part of your routine, away from the computer.

Planning and prioritizing often reduces or eliminates reactive behavior—which can include multi-tasking!

**What is the most helpful idea from this section?**

_____

_____

_____

_____

_____

_____

_____

_____

_____

_____

_____

_____

_____

_____

_____

## Take Frequent Breaks

Don't just think lunchtime will do as a break. If you spend your days sitting at a computer, schedule a break every hour (two at the max) and use a timer with an alarm to remind you, until it becomes a habit. Then get up. Walk around. Walk round the block. Do some exercises: Or just lie flat with your legs on a pillow, letting your mind wander and your back rest. Make the breaks short—ten to fifteen minutes, maximum.

When you go back to the computer, you may find that the break stopped you from going off on a tangent, getting too involved in extraneous research or gave you the perfect opening for your next video. Solutions may suddenly present themselves, or your day will just get back into focus, so you can zoom in on your priorities.

***If you're not convinced***: Before you try this, track and assess how much you actually accomplish during your regular week. Then add the breaks, track and assess. Was there a difference? Did you get more accomplished, even though you took breaks? The same? Less?

## Eat Healthy Snacks

As part of your morning routine, prepare or select healthy snacks to take with you. Protein bars, fresh fruit, fresh veggie sticks, cheese, mini one-serving cans of tuna, nuts—whatever takes your fancy.

Remember to include healthy drink options too—sachets of green tea, or water with lemon or lime.

## Start Your Day with a Balanced Breakfast

Many people like carbs or something "light" for breakfast—but your brain and energy levels will do better if you eat a breakfast that is balanced. That means including protein and fresh produce too.

If you really don't want to eat bacon and eggs, there are lots of healthier alternatives. A glass of milk or yogurt for protein; protein powder mixed in with porridge or with a smoothie; a protein bar plus an apple (that gives you all the protein and carbs you could want).

Adding spinach to your smoothie also gives you those crucial "leafy greens"—and you won't taste spinach. It becomes a neutral flavor in smoothies.

## Start Work at the Same Time Every Day

Even if you're self-employed and you live to be flexible, keep yourself to one set time slot—and that's starting work at the same time every day. No matter how flexible you are the rest of the day, getting yourself into the habit of sitting down to work at the same time every day will help you accomplish more—and avoid procrastination.

## Create Rewards in your Day

It's a well-known fact: If there's a reward at the end of a difficult road, people are far more likely to stay the course. What is your ideal reward for being productive?

Remember that rewards are not always tangible. While it's nice to eat a truffle every time you exceed seeing three clients a day, you can also indulge in rewards like using a Fitbit to measure the number of steps you take; or going for a swim, if you shave an hour off your work time.

The important thing is to identify the type of reward that would appeal to you—and set it up so you can achieve it. (It should be neither too unreachable nor too easy, for the best emotional impact.)

**What is the most helpful idea from this section?**

_____

_____

_____

_____

_____

_____

_____

_____

_____

_____

_____

_____

_____

_____

_____

_____

_____

_____

## Learn to Tune Yourself Up

You've likely made adjustments at the beginning of the day, but to make your morning routine extra-effective, get into the habit of stopping for a quick "tune up"—just after lunch is ideal.

Review where you are in your day. Exercise or meditate, if you need to. Refocus and tweak your day's calendar, if you've run into snags or miscalculations.

## Shorten Tasks You Find Difficult

If you know it's going to kill you if you exercise for fifteen minutes in the morning, exercise for five. If you know you're going to hate devoting a timed hour to cleaning out your inbox, just unsubscribe from six contacts; or delete twenty letters.

The important thing—especially if you're trying to take on a new resolution or activity—is to get into the habit of doing it first. (Worry about "how long" later, when the habit is firmly adopted!)

## Realize that "Urgent" is Not the Same as "Important"

Especially when the urgency is true for someone else—not you. Urgency is often unfortunately paired with reactivity: And that's a counter-productive state and trait.

## Switch Off Unnecessary Devices

Disconnect from the net and close your browsers unless you are actively researching or uploading/downloading. Turn off your phone. Concentrate only on your top priorities for the day—and don't turn your devices again until you're done.

## Keep Track of Ideas

When you're in a productive zone, ideas tend to fly at you out of nowhere. Make sure you devise and adopt a system to keep track of them: A physical notebook in your purse and one each beside your bed and favorite chair; an app such as Evernote on your computer or iPhone; even a Rolodex and index cards.

You may think you'll remember those ideas later, but it's a proven fact that most people don't: So make sure you catch them while they're hot!

## Give Yourself a Time Limit

If you often find that the more you try to complete something, the more work it seems to generate, meaning you never finish, then give yourself a time limit—and focus on meeting that deadline.

When you look at a big goal, it's common to get frustrated at the enormity of what you're trying to accomplish. If you wake up each day determined to spend it forming good habits, you give yourself a better chance at success. So use these success habits as a starting place to build a successful business and life.

**What is the most helpful idea from this section?**

_____

_____

_____

_____

_____

_____

_____

# FIVE FAVORITES

Automation is a good success and productivity habit to get into. So is taking shortcuts—as long as quality doesn't suffer.

Add these five sources of inspiration and information, and you're well on your way to a powered-up day. So let's take a look at resources that may help you accomplish all of this:

## #1. Evernote

The handy app that is so much more than simply a notebook. You can save images and voice messages, track tasks, "clip from anywhere on the web" and cloud-sync it between your PC and mobile. And you can share your Evernote items and discuss them too.

There are paid versions with even more features, but the Basic version that does everything listed above is free.

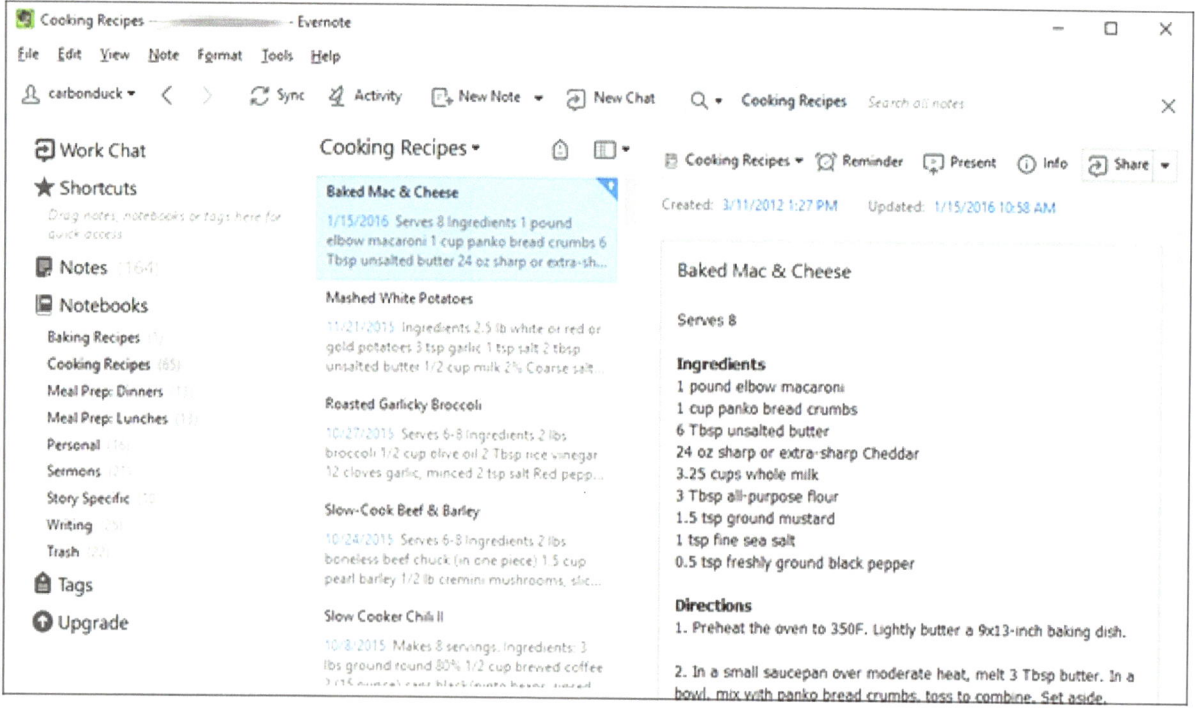

www.evernote.com

## #2. RescueTime

 If you work on the computer during the day, use an app such as RescueTime to help show you exactly how much time you're spending on billable or valuable work. RescueTime will deliver you a weekly report, showing in diagram form exactly where you spent your time.

Two tips, however: Be honest when telling it what sites you visit and why: And get the paid version (it's way more accurate—and only $9.00 per month; with four free months if you choose the annual-pay option).

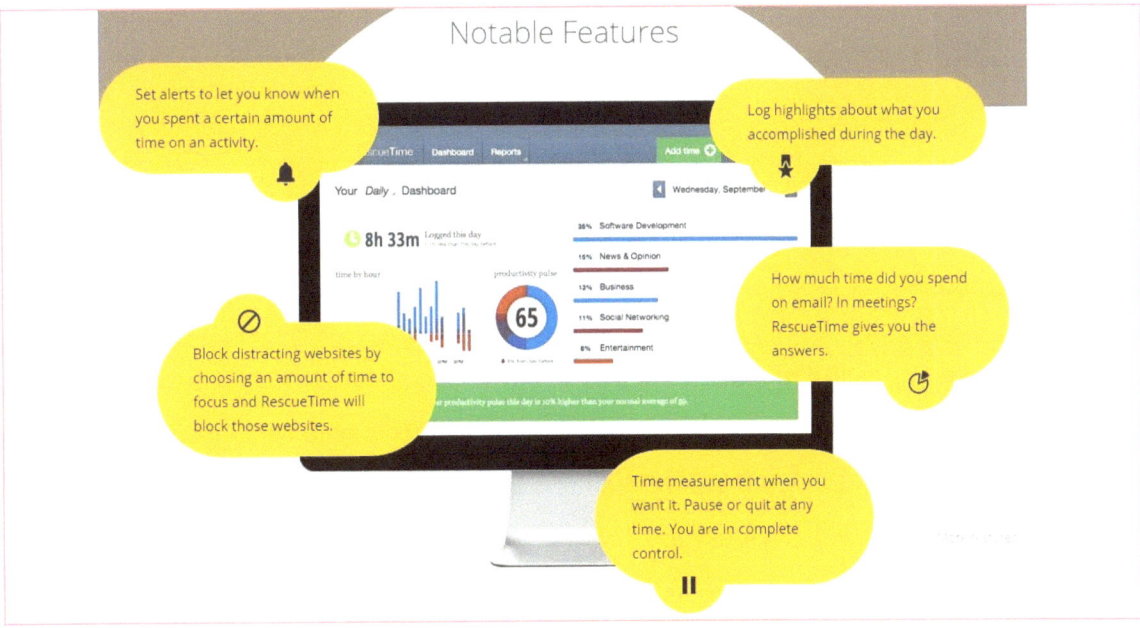

https://www.rescuetime.com/

## #3. The Positivity Blog

A great source of focused tips, inspiration and quick pick-me-ups from the incredibly wise Henrik Ekberg.

http://www.positivityblog.com/

## #4. Unroll.me

Identifies and puts your subscription emails into one email, so you can read them at once, at one time every day. It also intuitively categorizes them. And if you need to check a particular email, just look in the folder Unroll.me creates for you—it's called "Unroll Me". Works with mainstream email providers like Gmail and Yahoo.

And you can unsubscribe from any one (or many) of these emails with a simple click.

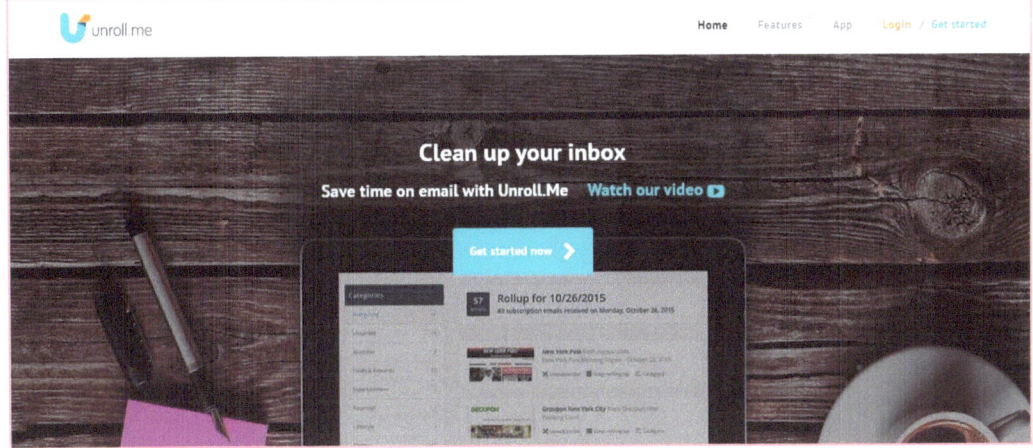

https://unroll.me


## #5. Audible

If you're an aural learner—if you like to listen rather than read or watch—take advantage of Audible's free trial.

Audible is an app that allows you to access a library of over 180,000 audiobooks on your mobile devices.

If you like it, you may agree that's well worth the $15.00 per month fee.

http://amzn.to/2eFgaMd

# Success Planning

Use the following pages to help establish and maintain a strong
routine to jump start your quarter.

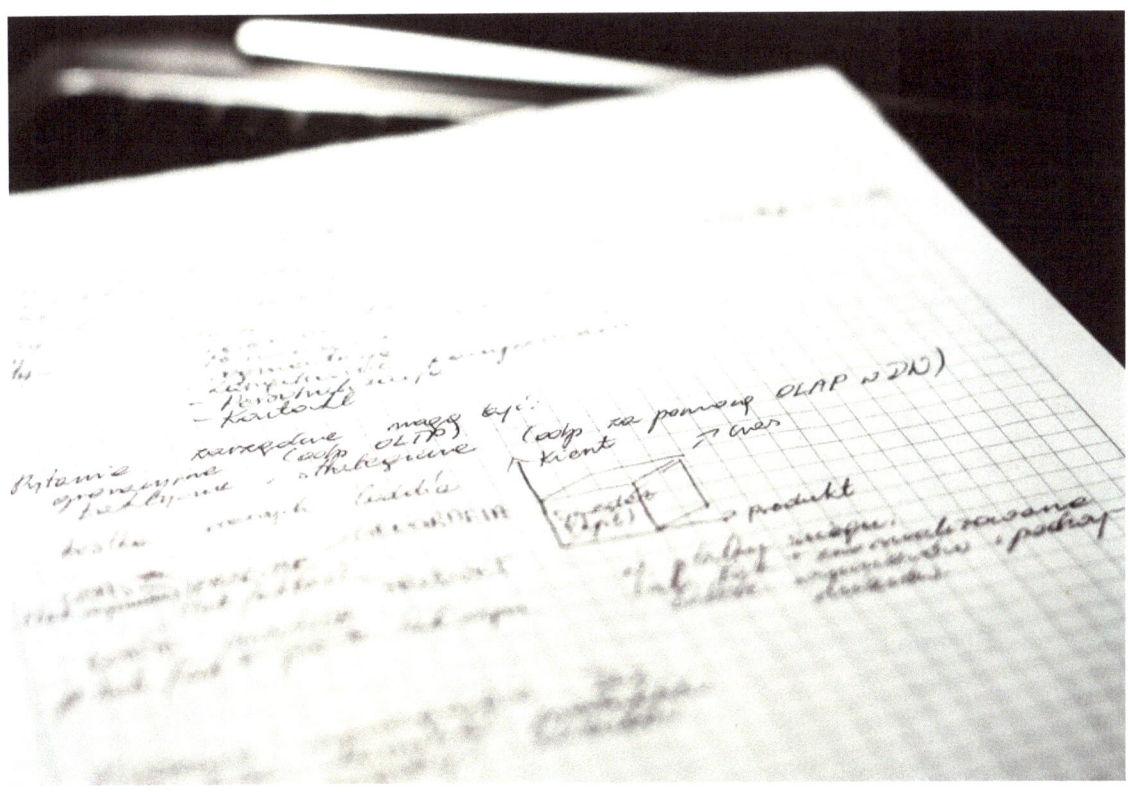

# Quarterly Action Plan for the Next 3 Months

| | |
|---|---|
| **Area Of Focus:** <br> (Branding, Selling ,Clients, Product Creation, Funding, etc.) | |
| **Goals** | 1. <br><br> 2. <br><br> 3. |
| **Action Steps** | |
| **Resources** | |

# 30 Minute Business Plan

**BUSINESS OVERVIEW**

**What will I sell?**

**Who will buy it?**

**How will my business help others?**

**PRICING STRATEGY**

**What will I charge for my products/services?**

**High End**

**Moderate Price**

**Budget**

What form of payment will I accept?

## MARKETING STRATEGY

How will customers/clients learn about my business?

## FINANCIAL PROJECTIONS

My business will be successful when it achieves…

Number of customers

Monthly Income

# Vision

Your vision is the key connector between your daily goals
and your lifetime purpose. Locate images and/ or words that
reflect your yearly business goals. Cut and paste them on this page.

# This Month's Goal _____

| | | | | | | |
|---|---|---|---|---|---|---|
| SUNDAY | MONDAY | TUESDAY | WEDNESD | THURSDAY | FRIDAY | SATURDAY |
| ☐ | ☐ | ☐ | ☐ | ☐ | ☐ | ☐ |
| ☐ | ☐ | ☐ | ☐ | ☐ | ☐ | ☐ |
| ☐ | ☐ | ☐ | ☐ | ☐ | ☐ | ☐ |
| ☐ | ☐ | ☐ | ☐ | ☐ | ☐ | ☐ |
| ☐ | ☐ | ☐ | ☐ | ☐ | ☐ | ☐ |

**Month:** _____

Use this form to keep track of key things that have happened to you and your business. It is for your eyes only. It may be helpful for you to refer to this form when preparing for next month.

**What successes have I experienced?**

_____

_____

_____

**What challenges have I experienced?**

_____

_____

_____

**What help do I need?**

_____

_____

_____

## This Month's Goal _____

| SUNDAY | MONDAY | TUESDAY | WEDNESD | THURSDAY | FRIDAY | SATURDAY |
|--------|--------|---------|---------|----------|--------|----------|
| | | | | | | |
| | | | | | | |
| | | | | | | |
| | | | | | | |
| | | | | | | |

**Month:** _____

Use this form to keep track of key things that have happened to you and your business. It is for your eyes only. It may be helpful for you to refer to this form when preparing for next month.

**What successes have I experienced?**

_____

_____

_____

**What challenges have I experienced?**

_____

_____

_____

**What help do I need?**

_____

_____

_____

## This Month's Goal _____

| SUNDAY | MONDAY | TUESDAY | WEDNESD | THURSDAY | FRIDAY | SATURDAY |
|--------|--------|---------|---------|----------|--------|----------|
| ☐ | ☐ | ☐ | ☐ | ☐ | ☐ | ☐ |
| ☐ | ☐ | ☐ | ☐ | ☐ | ☐ | ☐ |
| ☐ | ☐ | ☐ | ☐ | ☐ | ☐ | ☐ |
| ☐ | ☐ | ☐ | ☐ | ☐ | ☐ | ☐ |
| ☐ | ☐ | ☐ | ☐ | ☐ | ☐ | ☐ |

**Month:** _____

Use this form to keep track of key things that have happened to you and your business. It is for your eyes only. It may be helpful for you to refer to this form when preparing for next month.

**What successes have I experienced?**

_____

_____

_____

**What challenges have I experienced?**

_____

_____

_____

**What help do I need?**

_____

_____

_____

## Your Morning Routine

**Identify the habits from your morning routine that are distracting/not working for you/counter-productive.**

- ☐ Facebook
- ☐ Email
- ☐ Other social network: _____
- ☐ Playing a game
- ☐ Watching a TV show
- ☐ Sleeping in
- ☐ Other distracting habits:

_____

_____

_____

_____

_____

_____

**Identify the central problem that causes you to cling to these habits**

- ☐ Procrastination
- ☐ Boredom with work
- ☐ Feeling too unwell to work
- ☐ Feeling too tired to work
- ☐ Wanting to avoid work/certain tasks

_____

_____

_____

**What better habit can you replace truly energy-draining, avoidant or distracting habits with?**

**Start straight away in drinking one glass of water before you do anything else in your day. Is this habit easy to adopt? If not, what is keeping you from drinking water?**

- ☐ It makes me gag

- ☐ I crave coffee too badly

- ☐ I can't stand ice cold water

- ☐ I can't stand room temperature water

- ☐ It gives me heartburn

- ☐ Other

_____

_____

_____

_____

_____

_____

_____

_____

_____

**Determine what you can do to fix this—then do it!**

- [ ] Put ice in my morning water
- [ ] Add a slice of lemon or lime juice to my morning water (hint: Good for combatting heartburn)
- [ ] Add a drop of non-sugar flavoring to my morning water
- [ ] Drink sparkling water
- [ ] Drink bottled water
- [ ] Drink mineral water
- [ ] Other

_____

_____

_____

_____

_____

_____

**Decide how you can add exercise into your morning routine:**

- [ ] Go for a 15-20-minute walk
- [ ] Go for a ten-minute jog
- [ ] Do an exercise routine
- [ ] Follow an exercise tape or show
- [ ] Do yoga, tai chi or qi gong
- [ ] Us an app like the 7-minute Workout

- ☐ Add music to your morning exercise routine

- ☐ Do a household task like sweeping the floor; vacuuming

- ☐ Other

_____

_____

_____

_____

_____

_____

**Decide on something motivational or inspirational to add to your morning routine:**

- ☐ Practicing counting your blessings

- ☐ Choosing a daily affirmation or bible verse

- ☐ Reading an uplifting or educational article

- ☐ Listening to a motivating podcast

- ☐ Challenge yourself with a meaningful question of the day

- ☐ Spend time daydreaming with your vision board or adding new visualizations/goals

- ☐ Other

- ☐

_____

_____

_____

_____

**Plan a night routine that supports your morning routine:** Tick off any action that resonates with you as a good end-of-day strategy to aid you in keeping your new morning routine:

☐ Open your curtains or blinds, last thing before climbing into bed

☐ Set your alarm clock earlier than usual

☐ Prepare your priorities or to-do list after work

☐ Pre-prepare your smoothie, so that all you have to do is add ice or another key ingredient and remix

☐ Lay out your clothes for tomorrow

☐ Choose the article you will read; affirmation you want to adopt for the day/week or podcast you plan to listen to as part of your routine

☐ Other

_____

_____

_____

_____

_____

_____

**Write down your new morning routine in the space below.**

# End of the Quarter Review

What Did I Accomplish This Quarter?

What I Didn't Accomplish, But Intended To?

The Challenges and Problems am I Facing Now

What Opportunities Are Available To Me Right Now

List 3 Things You Can Improve On This Coming Quarter

What Concreate Actions Can You Take To Work Towards These Improvements?

# NOTES

# NOTES

# NOTES

# NOTES

NOTES

# NOTES

*My first training was awesome. I have the clarity
and resources to turn my purpose into a real
business.*

**Shannise J.** New Media Journalist

www.ingramcontent.com/pod-product-compliance
Lightning Source LLC
Chambersburg PA
CBHW050903180526
45159CB00007B/2771

* 9 7 8 1 5 3 9 6 9 6 7 5 9 *